The Wilderness Sanctuary

By

Susanna Roberts

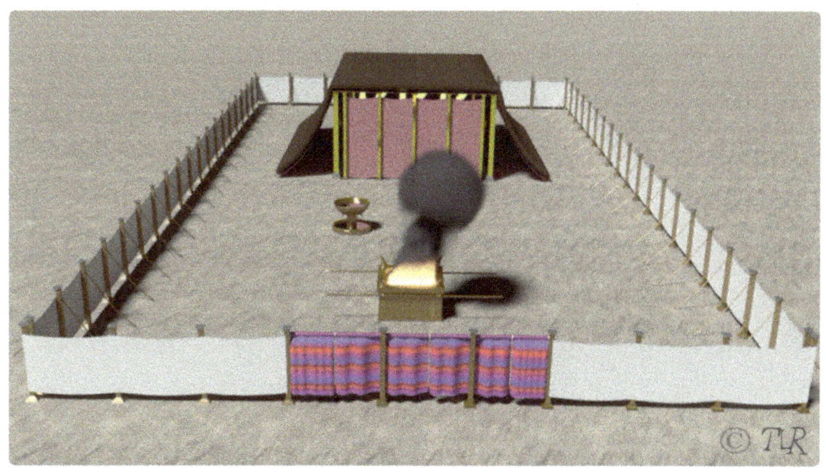

Illustrations by Trenton Roberts, Joe Maniscalco, Daniel Roberts, and Dallas Roberts

ISBN   978-0-9987695-0-9

Soon after they left Egypt, God gave Moses and the Israelites the plans for building a special tent. God said, *"Let them make me a sanctuary; that I may dwell among them."* (Exodus 25:8) The special tent was called the tabernacle or sanctuary.

The sanctuary on earth was a model or miniature. Maybe you have little model cars that look like the big cars your parents drive or miniature animal toys that look like real animals. The sanctuary the Israelites were to build was a little model of the sanctuary up in heaven.

1

The people were happy to give offerings to God. Fathers and mothers, boys and girls, brought many gifts so that they could build the sanctuary. They cheerfully brought linen cloth, ram's skins, and goat's hair. They brought jewels of gold and silver and special stones. Some of them brought brass and pieces of special wood, spices, and oil.

We should cheerfully give our offerings to Jesus too. These people were so happy to help that soon they had more than enough materials to build the sanctuary.

God gave the people knowledge and skill so that they could make the sanctuary beautiful. Women and men spun cloth and sewed special curtains. God picked two special men to build the furniture of the sanctuary. One was named Bezaleel and the other was named Aholiab.

God helped them know how to carve and build things out of wood, and how to make things out of metal. He also taught them how to cut and set stones. God helped them with everything they needed to know to build the sanctuary. God promises to help you learn too, if you'll ask Him.

Because the Israelites were traveling, God made the wilderness sanctuary so that it could be taken apart and put back together easily, like a tent for camping. Every time the Israelites stopped for a while they would set up the sanctuary.

When they traveled, they carried it with them. Some pieces were carried on their shoulders and some in ox carts. God picked out special people to help take care of the sanctuary. They were called Levites.

The sanctuary was divided into three main sections. It had a yard, just like your house probably does. It was called the courtyard. The courtyard was around the outside of the tent tabernacle.

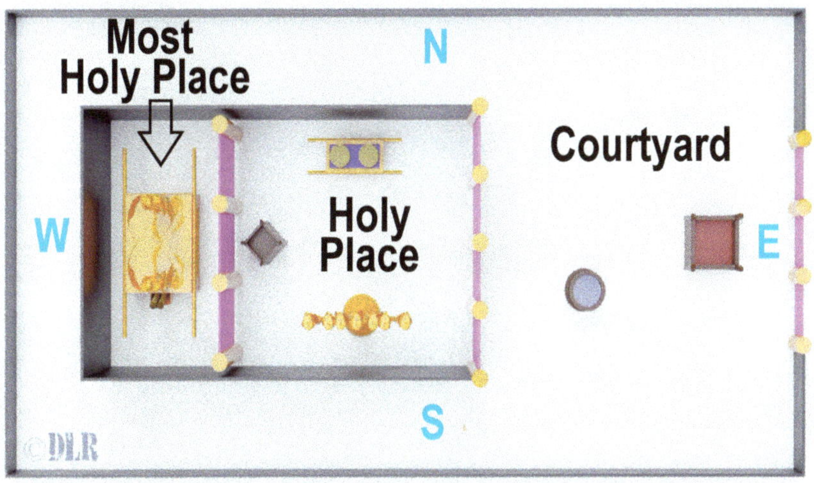

The tent tabernacle had only two rooms. One was called the Holy Place and the other one was called the Most Holy Place. There was a pretty curtain between the two rooms. When the Israelites set up the tabernacle, the Most Holy Place was always on the west. The west side is where you can see the pretty sunset at night.

The courtyard had a white curtain all around it. The curtain was made of linen, a special kind of cloth. The linen curtain was hung on brass pillars, like a fence on fence posts. Brass looks kind of like a shiny penny.

The courtyard was one hundred cubits long and fifty cubits wide. In Bible times, instead of using a ruler, they measured with their hands and arm.

A cubit was measured from a man's elbow to his fingertip.

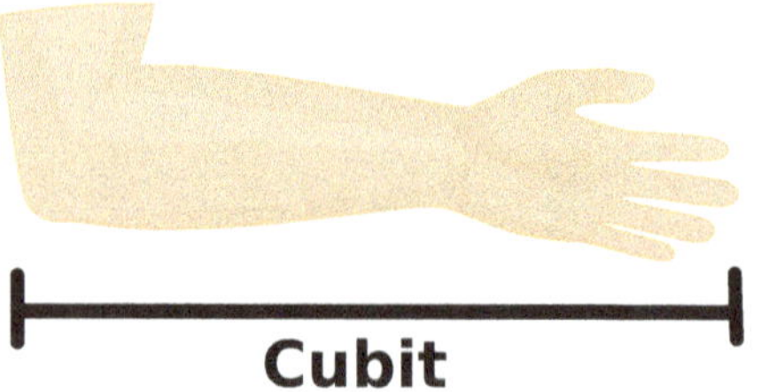

Each pillar, or fence post, in the court had a socket or base of brass. On top of the pillar was a little hat or chapiter that was made of silver. Silver looks a lot like a shiny spoon or fork.

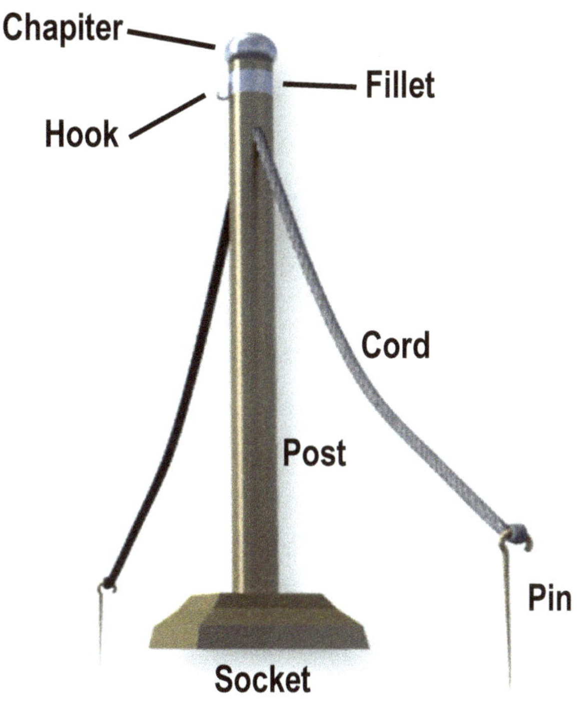

The posts had fillets and hooks that were also made of silver. Pins of brass were used in the ground like tent stakes with cords or ropes to help keep the posts standing up straight.

Just like Jesus is the only way to heaven, there was only one way into the courtyard. Jesus said, *"I am the way, the truth, and the life: no man cometh unto the Father, but by me."* (John 14:6) The gate was on the east end of the courtyard. East is where the sun comes up in the morning.

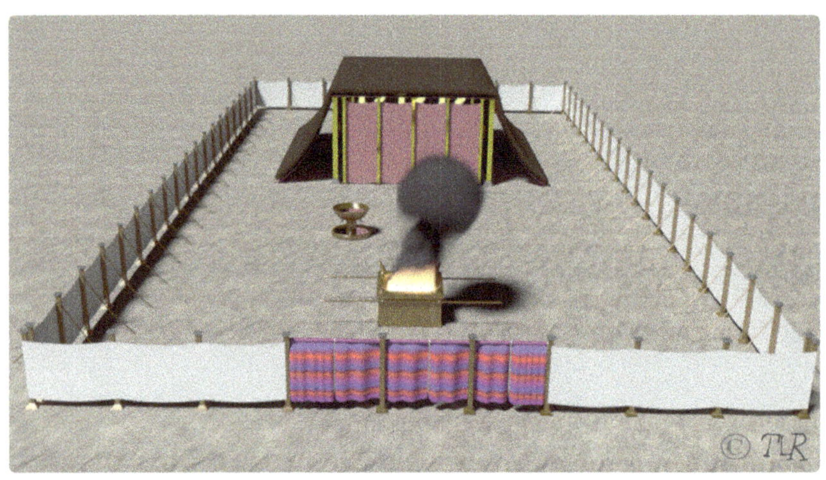

The gate was 20 cubits wide. It was hung on four brass pillars just like the rest of the courtyard. The curtains of the gate were made of white, blue, purple, and bright red, called scarlet. The curtains were decorated with special needlework.

In the courtyard there were two pieces of furniture. The first piece of furniture was called the altar of burnt offering. It was kind of like a woodstove or a fireplace because a fire was always burning on it.

When the people did something wrong a lamb had to be slain and offered on the altar. This reminded the people that one day Jesus, the "Lamb of God," would die to take away their sins. I'm glad that Jesus died for us and rose again so that we can go to heaven one day.

The altar was square and made of wood that was covered with brass. The altar was hollow inside. In the middle was a grate for the fire to sit on. The altar had horns on the four corners of it.

It had special pots, shovels and fleshhooks that were also made of brass.

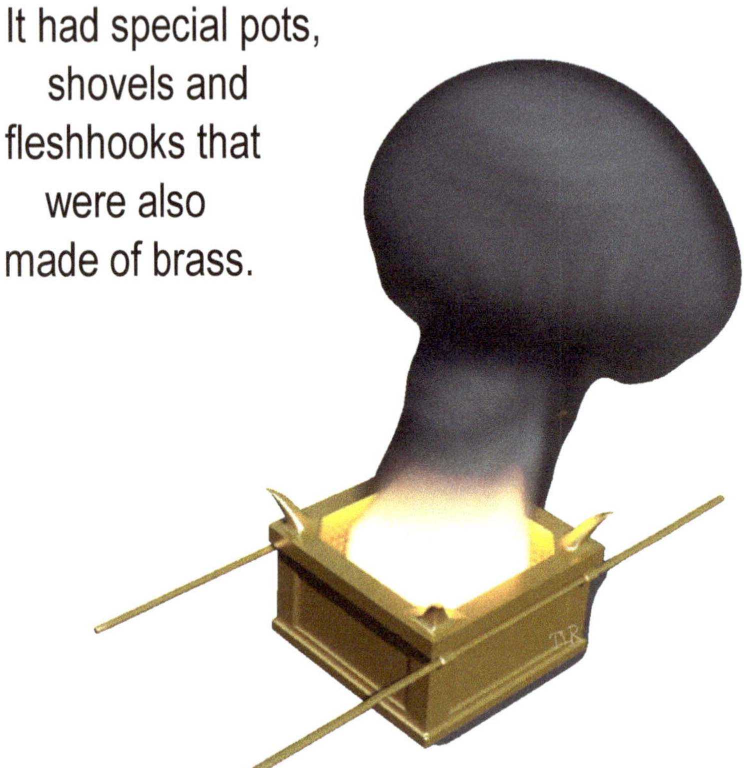

The altar had four brass rings that were hooked on to it. These rings were used to hold the special sticks called staves so that the altar could be carried.

The next piece of furniture in the courtyard was a laver. It was kind of like a big wash basin. Both the laver and its foot, or base, were made of brass. It was made out of the mirrors that the women had cheerfully given to help build the sanctuary.

The priests used the water to wash some of the animals that were used for sacrifices. They also used the water in the laver to wash themselves. They had to take off their shoes and wash their hands and feet before they could go into the tabernacle tent.

At the front opening of the tabernacle tent there were five pillars. These pillars had sockets or bases of brass. The pillars were made of wood covered in gold. The pillars stood up firm and straight. Just like the pillars stood straight and firm, boys and girls who love Jesus are to stand firmly for what is right and good.

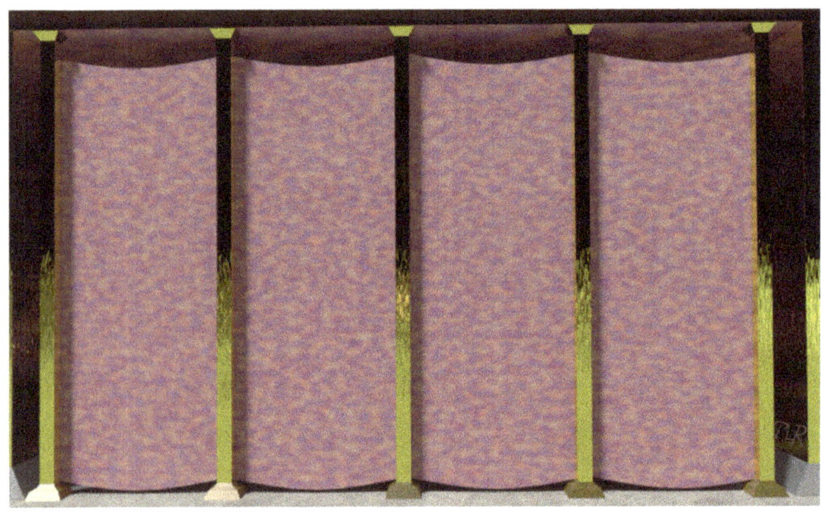

A beautiful curtain was hung from these five pillars. Like the curtain at the gate, it was made of fine linen colored white, blue, purple, and bright red, called scarlet. It had even fancier patterns of needlework.

Only the priests went inside the tabernacle tent.
Every day the priest went into the Holy Place.
The Holy Place had three special pieces of
furniture. A special table called
the table of showbread was on the north side of
the Holy Place.

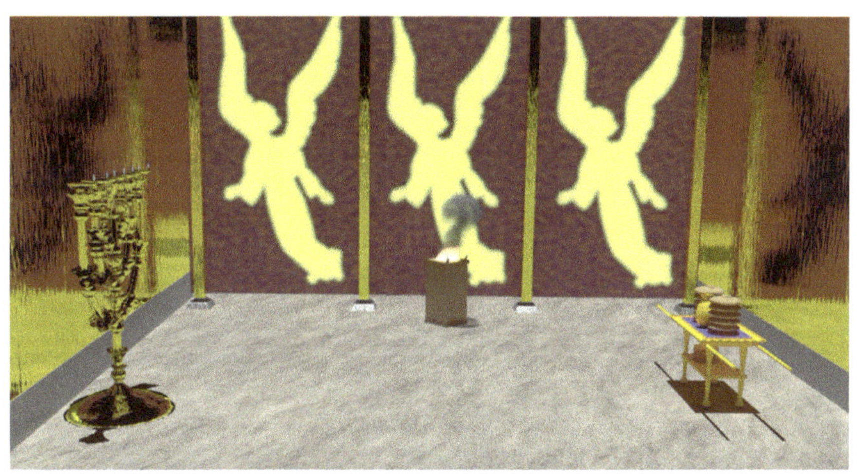

The table was made of wood that was covered in
gold. It had golden crown decorations on it.
It also had four rings hooked on it, and it had
special sticks or staves for the Levites to carry it
with when they traveled.

On top of the table of showbread there was a cloth of blue. And just like most tables, the table of showbread had dishes and spoons. It also had twelve loaves of unleavened bread on top of it. Frankincense was sprinkled on the top of the two stacks of bread.

The bread reminds us of Jesus, because Jesus said *"I am the bread of Life."* The bread also reminds us of the Bible because Jesus said, *"man shall not live by bread alone, but by every word of God."* (Luke 4:4) Just like we need to eat each day, we need to study the Bible and learn about Jesus every day too, so we can grow to be strong, healthy Christians.

Across from the table of showbread was the golden candlestick. It had seven branches, and it was made from one talent of gold that had been beaten into the shape of a candlestick. It was decorated with almond-shaped bowls, knops, and flowers.

The candlestick was filled with oil, and it made light in the Holy Place. The priests were never to let this light go out. The light reminds us of Jesus, because Jesus said, *"I am the light of the world."*

When we follow Jesus, we can be little lights too. We can let our light shine by telling other boys and girls and friends about Jesus.

On the side of the Holy Place farthest from the door, we find the altar of incense. It was made of wood covered in gold. It was decorated with a crown, and it had four horns on the corners.

Every morning and evening the priest burned incense of sweet spices and frankincense on it. The smell reminded them of how sweet it is to trust in Jesus and pray to Him each day.

Behind the altar of incense was a special veil curtain. It was hung on four pillars. Like the walls of the tabernacle, the pillars were wood covered in gold. The walls and the pillars had sockets, or bases, that were made of silver.

The special curtain was hung from golden hooks. It divided the Holy Place from the Most Holy Place. Like the other curtains, the veil was white, blue, purple and scarlet, but this one had pictures of angels sewn into it, making it even more special. The angels remind us of our guardian angels that Jesus sends to take care of us.

When Jesus died on the cross to save us from our sins, this veil was ripped in half from the top to the bottom.
Because we have all sinned and been naughty, Jesus had to die so that there was a way for us to

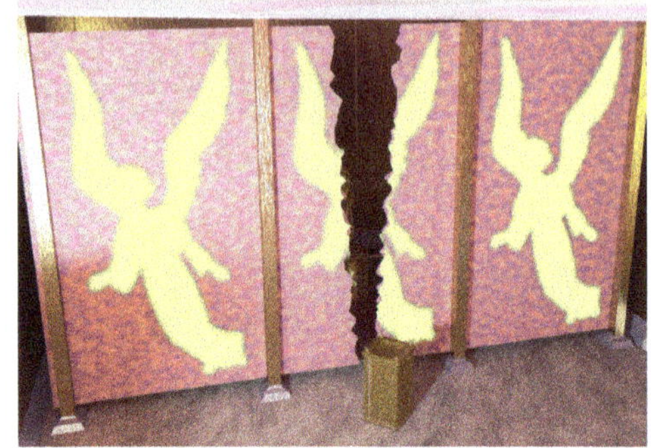

be able to go to heaven.

The angels on the special curtain also remind us of the three special angels found in the Bible book called Revelation. Those angels tell us to worship Jesus who created the world for us. They also tell us

that *"the hour of his judgment is come."*
Judgment time is like the Day of Atonement.

No one ever went into the Most Holy Place except the high priest. And he only went in there once a year on the Day of Atonement. On the Day of Atonement, the high priest went into the Most Holy Place and sprinkled blood on the mercy seat seven times. While the high priest was doing his work inside the tabernacle, the people were also to do some special things.

Jesus is our High Priest. When Satan says we don't deserve heaven, Jesus says He died in our place. When we are truly sorry for our sins, and ask Jesus to help us be good, Jesus promises to forgive our sins.

The ark of the covenant and the mercy seat were the only pieces of furniture in the Most Holy Place. The ark was like a wooden box. It was covered on the inside and on the outside with gold. It had a golden crown decoration on it.

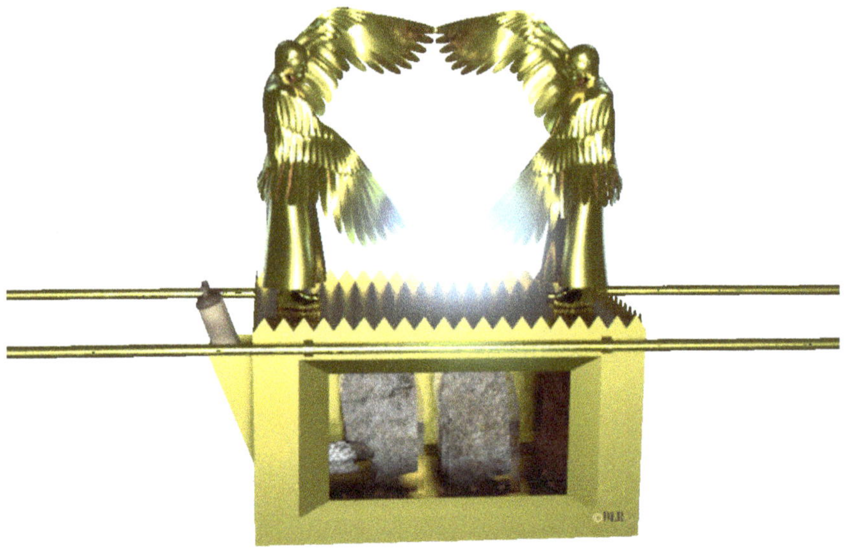

The ark had four golden rings hooked to it, and it had gold covered staves for carrying it. These were not to be taken out, because nobody was supposed to touch the ark or they would die. When the priests carried the ark they covered it with a special blue cloth.

On top of the ark sat the mercy seat. It was made of pure gold. It had two golden angels on it at either end. They were facing each other looking toward the mercy seat.

Over the mercy seat is where God put the special light of His presence that showed He was with the children of Israel.

Jesus wants to live in your heart too, if you will ask Him to come in.

The ark of the covenant held some special things. Inside you could find God's law—the Ten Commandments written on stone, a bowl of the manna that God sent from heaven, and Aaron's rod that budded and grew almonds.

On the side of the ark was a special place for the book of the law. These things remind us that we are to hide God's Word and His law in our hearts. Aaron's rod that budded reminds us of the promises in God's word—like the hope of again seeing those who died loving Jesus, when Jesus comes to take us to heaven.

The roof of the tabernacle tent wasn't quite like your house. Instead it was made up of four different layers. On the outside was a waterproof layer made of animal skins. Inside this was a rams' skin colored red.

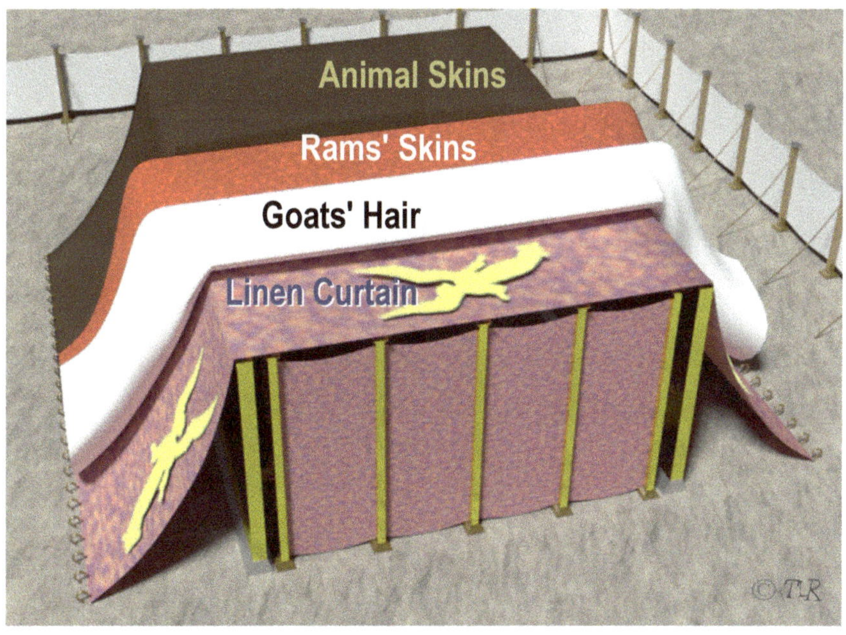

The next layer was made of goats' hair. And on the very inside was a beautiful curtain made of fine linen of white, blue, purple and scarlet linen. Like the veil inside, it was made with needlework that looked like angels.

God told Moses that the high priest was to wear special clothes when he worked in the sanctuary.

Like the other priests, he wore a white linen robe with white linen breeches that were kind of like shorts underneath it. Over his white robe he wore a blue robe with pomegranates and golden bells along the bottom. The little bells made tinkling sounds when he walked. He also wore a linen ephod that was kind of like a sleeveless vest and he wore a girdle or belt of white, gold, blue, purple and scarlet.

The high priest also wore a special hat or miter. It was a white linen turban. Connected to it by a lace of blue was a gold plate with the words on it, *"Holiness to the Lord."*

The words on this special hat remind us that

whatever we do, we should be thinking of Jesus. When we are playing with our friends, we should be like Jesus. When we are eating our food, we should be like Jesus. When we are choosing what to wear, we should be like Jesus. When we are doing our chores, we should be like Jesus. We should be like Jesus anytime, every time and all the time.

On the shoulders of the high priest were two onyx stones that had the names of the twelve tribes of Israel carved in them. The breastplate hung from these stones by golden chains and laces of blue.

The breastplate had twelve stones on it, one for each tribe of Israel.

It also had the Urim and the Thummim stones that God used to talk to the Israelites. The 12 special stones remind us of the New Jerusalem that is in heaven. The breastplate helps us to remember that even though Jesus is in heaven now, He is always thinking about us, and wants us to be with Him.

The wilderness sanctuary is a picture story to show us God's plan to save us from sin and how He wants to take us to heaven one day soon. The Bible says, *"Thy way, O God, is in the sanctuary: who is so great a God as our God?"* (Psalm 77:13)

The sanctuary reminds us of Jesus' love for us. It reminds us that He loved us enough to die for us so that He could save us from our sins. I want to show Jesus how much I love him by keeping His commandments, don't you?

Additional Teacher's Helps

The Sanctuary Path

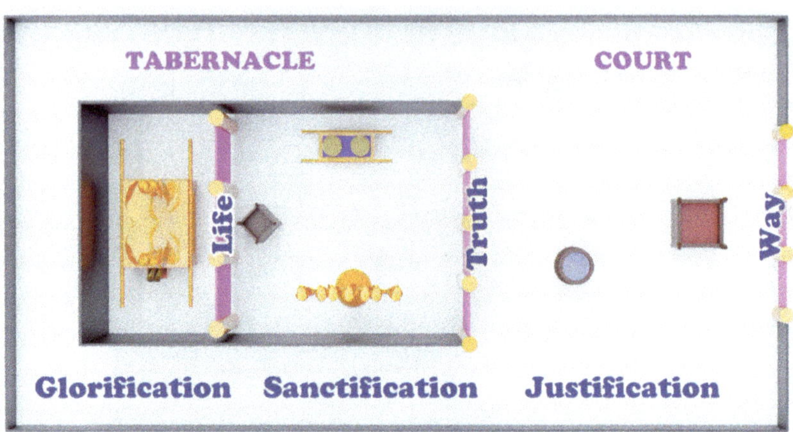

"Jesus saith unto him, I am the way, the truth, and the life: no man cometh unto the Father, but by me." John 14:6
"I am the door: by me if any man enter in, he shall be saved..."
John 10:9

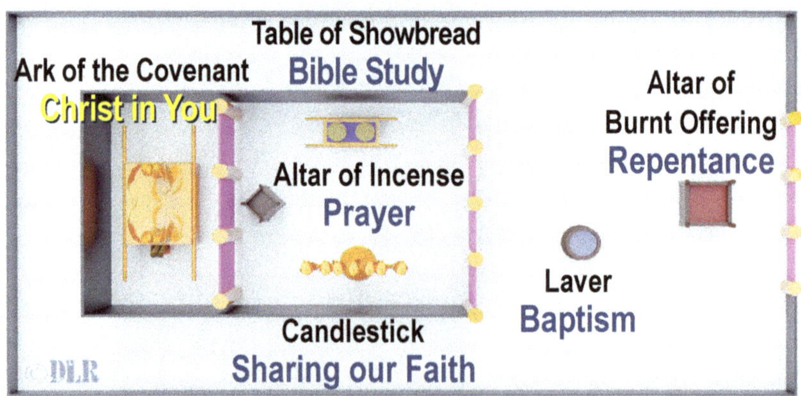

Repentance—Acts 3:19, 1 John 1:9 **Baptism**—Acts 2:38; Acts 22:16
Bible Study—2 Timothy 2:15; John 5:39 **Sharing Our Faith**—Matthew 5:16; Ephesians 5:8 **Prayer**—Revelation 8:3,4; 1 Thessalonians 5:17
Christ in You the Hope of Glory—Colossians 1:27; Jeremiah 31:33

Additional Teacher's Helps, Continued

Bible Measures

Additional Teacher's Helps, Continued

Waymarks of Truth as found in the Pillars of the Sanctuary

Pillars of Christianity

4 Pillars at the Gate, Brass Pillars, Brass Sockets
Genesis 1, Genesis 3, Exodus 20, Romans 6:23/John 3:16

Pillars of the Reformation

5 Pillars at Tabernacle Entrance, Gold Pillars, Brass Sockets
Ephesians 2:8,9; Jeremiah 9:23,24/1 Corinthians 10:31;1 Timothy 2:5/John 14:6;
Isaiah 8:20/Acts 17:11/John 17:17; Romans 1:17/Hebrews 11:6

Additional Teacher's Helps, Continued

Waymarks of Truth as found in the Pillars of the Sanctuary

Last Day Pillars

4 Pillars at the Entry to the Most Holy Place
Gold Pillars, Silver Sockets

Revelation 14:6-12;
John 14:15; Exodus 20:8-11; Exodus 31:13; Ecclesiastes 20:12,20;
Psalm 115:17; Eccl. 9:5,6,10; 1 Thess.4:13-18; Daniel 12:2; John 5:28,29
Hebrews 8,9; Daniel 8:14

"Remove not the ancient landmark, which thy fathers have set."
Proverbs 22:28

www.ingramcontent.com/pod-product-compliance
Lightning Source LLC
Chambersburg PA
CBHW041034100825
30899CB00008B/49